# Echoes of Trinity Site

by

## Jim Clayton

**FIRST EDITION**

Copyright 1996, by Jim Clayton
Library of Congress Catalog Card No: 94-90888
ISBN: 1-56002-552-2

**UNIVERSITY EDITIONS, Inc.**
**59 Oak Lane, Spring Valley**
**Huntington, West Virginia 25704**

erek Clayton

# Dedication

There have been so many people who have touched my life in profound and enriching ways that dedicating this book to only one person first seemed like an impossible dilemma. I agonized over this issue for a long time. I finally chose to dedicate this book to two of the many people who have been, in some indirect way, responsible for this book.

I dedicate this book to Pat Cook without whose counsel I would never have spread my wings nor would I have had the self esteem necessary to face the challenges of compiling this book. Her counsel has led me to where I am, both spiritual and physical, and provided me with the opportunity to write this book. Thank you Pat.

I would also like to dedicate this book to John Hitchcock, a dear friend and mentor. By the mere presence of John in my life and by the model he offered me, I was challenged to write well. Thank you John just for being you and for sharing part of your life with me.

Jim Clayton

"Once asked, a question can never be forgotten. As long as humans have existed, someone has asked 'what if?' "

"But too often the question 'Is war acceptable' is confused with the question 'What kind of war is acceptable' and this nefariously clouds the issue."

"So many questions, not enough answers. Child age 11"

"It all makes you stop and think, doesn't it?"

# ECHOES OF TRINITY SITE

It has been fifty years since the first atomic explosion at Trinity Site near Alamogordo, New Mexico. The momentous explosion on July 16, 1945 still echoes around the world fifty years later. That historic event led to the delivery of two atomic bombs to Hiroshima and Nagasaki, ending the most devastating war in the history of the world.

The course of history was forever changed by the discovery of the atomic bomb. Some may say that the change was not for the better. Many believe otherwise. The Cold War and the evolution of Europe certainly would have been dramatically different if the atomic bomb were never developed. The nature of the war in the Pacific would have been forever altered without the atomic bomb and the subsequent historical, social and economic development of Japan was forever altered.

And America lived through the period of "Duck and Cover" in the late 1940s and through the 1950s. What kind of effect did that era have upon the psychological makeup of the children growing up then and upon their children and grandchildren? It must be nothing less than profound.

The concept of war was also forever changed. Who can say how the Korean War or the war in Vietnam would have evolved if the threat of atomic bombs did not exist? Who can say that there would not have been more wars or less wars or more costly wars if atomic bombs were not part of the equation?

International relations have never been the same. Atomic discoveries forever changed the nature of international relationships. The old order was gone. Who can say that the old order would not have continued if the atomic energy was never discovered? And medical and industrial development has also been significantly and forever changed due to atomic discoveries.

There are probably only a handful of people in the world who are unaware of the significance of the atomic age. It is a rare person indeed who does not harbor deep and profound attitudes toward the atomic bomb and atomic energy. It is these attitudes which are the echoes of that momentous occasion on July 16, 1945.

This book is an echo of that pivotal event.

# ACKNOWLEDGEMENTS

I wish to acknowledge the cooperation of John S. Rhoades, Director of the Bradbury Science Museum, in helping me to produce this book. I also wish to thank the staff at the Bradbury Science Museum for their gracious cooperation, especially Mary Ellen Ortiz.

I especially wish to acknowledge The Los Alamos Study Group who sponsored the exhibit from which this material was gathered. Without their exhibit this book would not exist and without the foresight of John S. Rhoades the exhibit itself would not exist.

I also wish to acknowledge the thousands of people who provided their comments in the log books at the Bradbury Science Museum and from which the primary content of this book was developed.

I wish to gratefully acknowledge the assistance of several people who translated the foreign text. My dear friend, Carol Hamblin, was instrumental in getting a Latvian translation for me direct from Latvia where she was serving in the Peace Corps.

I am most grateful for the translation assistance provided by Chigusa Yasuda, a student at the University of New Mexico. She provided the Japanese translations and enlisted the assistance of associates in the language department for the Korean and Chinese translations. The translation from Greek text was provided by Jennifer Hernandez also from the University of New Mexico. Professor Carolyn Simmons of the University of New Mexico is credited with translating the European languages.

Photographs in this book were taken by Eric Neilson of Taos, New Mexico.

The cover was designed by my son, Derek Clayton.

# TABLE OF CONTENTS

# INTRODUCTION

The Bradbury Science Museum in Los Alamos, New Mexico, houses a collection of exhibits which provide the public with information as to the past and present works of the Los Alamos National Laboratory (LANL). The historical significance of the Los Alamos National Laboratory is familiar to many people. It is there where in 1943, the first atomic bomb began development under the guidance of Dr. Robert Oppenheimer.

The facilities have existed ever since that time. From a laboratory which was once dedicated solely to nuclear development, it has become a scientific research facility which delves into other scientific arenas unrelated to nuclear physics. Its current mission involves the Laboratory in research dealing with AIDS, global climate warming, biotechnology as well as United States Defense Industry needs and dozens of other areas of research as well.

Los Alamos was a "closed city" up until 1957. Beginning in 1958, tours of Los Alamos were provided on a limited basis. The predecessor to the current museum originated with the efforts of Los Alamos National Laboratory Community Relations Director Robert Y. Porton. The original museum opened in the fall of 1963. In the first year, 14,000 visitors came to the Bradbury Science Museum from 50 states and 40 foreign countries. Today the Bradbury Science Museum receives about 80,000 visitors a year.

The Museum presents in pictures, exhibits, video presentations and hands-on experiments, the mission of the Los Alamos National Laboratory. It also provides scientific information on the environment as well. The material in the Museum is much more diverse in content than might be suspected especially since the Museum is so closely associated with the Los Alamos National Laboratory.

Not everyone, however, agrees with the mission of the Los Alamos National Laboratory nor with the work that has gone on in the past.

An organization called the Los Alamos Study Group requested that a portion of the Museum be set aside for "Healthy Disagreement" and "Alternative Perspectives". The group's wish was granted and a portion of the Museum was set aside for that purpose.

At this specific exhibit (referred to as "The Wall"), pictures and displays provide some views on the problems and dangers of nuclear research as well as some historical perspectives on the development of the atomic bomb including some dissenting views related to the decision to drop atomic bombs on Japan in 1945. As part of this exhibit, there is a plaque which reads:

## HEALTHY DISAGREEMENT

**The exhibit on this wall has been designed and produced by a group of citizens who disagree with the aspects of the Laboratory's past and current research.**

## ALTERNATIVE PERSPECTIVE

**The Bradbury Science Museum has made this space available to this group to encourage responsible debate about the role and future of this Laboratory.**

Below this plaque is a ledger (or log book) provided for the public so that they may write their comments about the Museum, the Laboratory, or anything else that might suit their fancy. They are free to write anything they wish. (Only a few abuse this privilege by writing obscenities and graffiti.)

The first ledger is 14" by 17" and consists of 152 pages of commentary. This ledger had its initial entry on April 4, 1993. The second ledger is 11" by 14" and consists of 186 pages. Ledger three and four are also 11" by 14" consisting of 200 pages each. As of July, 1994, ledger four is still active and not yet full. A page in any one of these ledgers may contain anywhere from one entry/comment to fifteen or more comments. Based on a cursory calculation, the average page contains ten commentaries. As of July, 1994, there were roughly 6,000 entries in these ledgers and it is growing daily. Some comments consist of one or two words and some fill most of a page and may consist of 100 or more words.

The type of people writing in these books could not be more diverse. There are children and adults, high school students, World War II veterans as well as children and grandchildren of World War II veterans. There are retired people, educators, people with PhDs, and ordinary people. There are the literate and semi-illiterate as well as people who fancy themselves as humorists. There are people associated with the Laboratory as well as those who have identified themselves as having been directly involved with the development of the atomic bomb. There are residents of Los Alamos, Santa Fe and other parts of New Mexico. There are visitors from Connecticut, New York, Wisconsin, Hawaii and Washington. There are many foreign visitors including those from Canada, Korea, Japan, Germany, China, Switzerland, New Zealand, USSR, England, Ireland, Latvia, Poland, France, Bosnia and the Ukraine. There are people who have openly identified themselves as doctors, artists and scientists. And there are those who have visited Hiroshima and Nagasaki and Dresden and Tokyo.

This, then, is a brief introduction to Los Alamos, the National Laboratory, the Bradbury Science Museum and the Los Alamos Study Group. For more information on any of these, refer to the Bibliography and reference list in the back of this book. Or, better yet, visit the Bradbury Science Museum in Los Alamos, New Mexico. There is a nearby bookstore where you will find dozens of books about all subjects related to Los Alamos, nuclear research, the atomic bomb and the people involved in the development of nuclear energy.

# FOREWORD

On my first visit to the Bradbury Science Museum I leafed through one of the ledgers and I was struck by the profound nature of many of those comments. I wanted to stay there and read them all. Some comments were funny, some cute, some profane, some irreverent, some irrelevant, some historical, some obnoxious and some even interesting and clever. After returning to Taos, New Mexico, the log books weighed heavily on my mind. I quickly drew the conclusion that there was contained in these ledgers a book begging to be published. I decided to extract what I thought to be the most interesting comments to produce that book. This, then, is the product of my dream and my efforts.

This book is really a Vox Populi book. What you will read are comments from ordinary citizens like yourself; comments which you may have written yourself had you been there and seen the exhibits. You will find yourself laughing at some, disagreeing with some, agreeing with others and perhaps getting quite angry over others. Hopefully you will laugh at the ones I found funny, find profound the ones I found profound, and perhaps you might even shed a tear over the poignant ones.

I had hoped to produce a book free of bias. I wanted to produce a book which contained no political slant—no bias. I wished to avoid either endorsing or denigrating the Museum, the Laboratory, Los Alamos or the Los Alamos Study Group. I also wanted to exclude any of my own personal opinions or feelings that I have on the related subjects. (I deliberately excluded the comments that I myself had written in the ledgers.) My objective was total neutrality. Hopefully I have succeeded in accomplishing my objective. I hope that you will be as entertained, provoked and intrigued by these commentaries as I was.

I'm sure that there will be those readers who will conclude that my efforts at fairness and objectivity have failed. I'm certain that there will be those who will accuse me of bias. There are those who will go to the effort of counting the number of quotes which are slanted one way or the other and conclude that

58% were pro-nuclear (or anti-nuclear) therefore proving my bias. As one commentator wrote, "You're damned if you do and damned if you don't."

I have divided the commentaries into what I feel are appropriate chapters representing different sentiments. Originally, I had about forty categories and chapters in mind and felt that was a few too many. I originally had a chapter devoted to comments from foreign visitors. I concluded that it would be best to integrate such comments into the sections which reflected their particular sentiment. I also originally had a chapter dedicated to "The Bomb" and another dedicated to LANL. I eliminated these chapters and moved the material to other, more appropriate chapters. I have since concluded that writing a book of this type is actually more difficult and time consuming than writing a novel.

The various chapters are somewhat arbitrary. Perhaps you may feel that some comments belong in a chapter other than the ones in which they appear. Perhaps some readers may conclude that some of the material I have included should not have been included in the first place. Your comments are welcome. You may write to me in care of the publisher or in care of the Bradbury Science Museum. If a sequel to this book is developed your suggestions may be incorporated.

I was faced with several enigmatic decisions. One decision was whether to present the quotes with no comments at all. I concluded that some commentary or explanation was necessary for many of them. Secondly, I wondered whether I should present the quotes exactly as they appeared, with their errors in spelling, punctuation, etc. I decided that the proper course was to correct the spelling and punctuation errors as long as such changes did not alter the intended message.

I also decided to leave the material as close to the original as possible with the exception that I have made minor alterations in some cases where the material would not otherwise be clear. I wished to leave the material as free as possible from a lot of imbedded editorial comments.

The direct quotes taken from the ledgers are presented in standard type. My comments are presented in italics. All material appearing within brackets [] are editorial or clarification commentary by me. Where the original material contained quotation marks, such marks are included. Where the original author has included underlining or other marks, such marks have also been reproduced. In some cases, however, some parts are not reproduced, such as triple underlining where the author intended to provide a great deal of emphasis. In any case, no matter what I might have done, some of the impact of a quotation will be lost when translating it from the handwritten form to a book.

In some cases an author of a comment included their name. It was not possible to acknowledge the name of the author of a quote in producing this book. In many cases the person's home state was included by the author. I decided to omit the state in most cases because it did not necessarily add to the significance of the individual comment. I have, however, included any identification of foreign countries since I believe that the ultimate significance of such commentaries is affected by such identification.

I suggest that readers not be too picky. In some cases people spelled "Nuclear Energy" and "Atomic Bomb" with capital letter and sometimes without. I have tried to include the original representation, although my research has revealed that "nuclear energy" and "atomic bomb" should not normally be capitalized.

In some cases the author wrote the whole comment in capital letters. I suspect that in many cases people did so because that is their normal way of writing. Where it was obvious that the use of capital letters was intended to add extra emphasis I have dutifully reproduced the material accordingly. Where it was not so obvious, I reproduced the quote in normal type.

Another issue should be raised. Again it is a matter of being too picky with the comments or their authors. The authors of each commentary had limited time and no benefit of a word processor nor dictionary. Do not judge harshly those comments which might not be up to your editorial standards. The comments are ad libs by their authors and should be judged according to their natural merits.

Where a comment was written in a foreign language, I have provided a reproduction of that comment as well as a translation. Translations were done by various people and agencies most of which have been identified in the acknowledgements at the beginning of this book.

There was plenty of material to choose from. Not all of the comments, however, were worthy of reproduction. However, many comments were omitted in this first edition simply because this book would be too large if all worthy comments were reproduced here. (Perhaps some day a sequel to this book will be produced.)

If the reader is intrigued by this subject as I have been and is interested in learning more about the Bradbury Science Museum, Los Alamos, LANL, or the people involved, then I encourage you to read any of the countless books on related subjects. A bibliography is provided at the end of this book. You may also write to the Bradbury Science Museum, the Los Alamos National Laboratory or the Los Alamos Study Group for more information. Mailing addresses are provided in the appendix of this book.

# PROLOGUE

*On an inside cover in the first ledger the following profound comments appear:*

The comments in this book are infinitely more interesting & educational and reveal more about human nature, than the exhibit with which it is associated.

The world is indeed changing and in response we too must change.

> Siegfried S. Hecker,
> Director
> Los Alamos National
> Laboratory
> 1986-present

*I stumbled upon some of my favorite comments after I had already collected most of the quotes that I had intended to publish. The following quotes really touched me.*

Some interesting reading here—A nice forum. Why not publish a collection of these comments ($)?

I think you should publish this book—AS IS—

Why not publish copies of the better written writings from this book?

# VISITOR COMMENTS

# THE BRADBURY SCIENCE MUSEUM

*This chapter contains quotes specifically about the Bradbury Science Museum.*

Great museum! Really shows the complexity of thought and scientific resources needed to work on a project—and a nuclear project especially. Hopefully nuclear power and other applications will bring a better future for all mankind.

An afternoon well worth the drive here.

The "alterative" wall is <u>wonderful!</u> Good for you for including it.

Thank you John Rhoades—4/2/93 Los Alamos Study Group.

This is one of the most interesting museums I have been in. Should be a must for all school children.

We especially enjoyed your exhibits on Marie Curie and the Russian gift. The exhibits were amazing and touched us immensely. The cost of this project (this building) was well spent and seems to be carefully considering the public's questions and opinion. We appreciate all the work that was put into it.

Middle School,
Denver School of the
Arts

P.S. The exhibit concerning the reverse side of Los Alamos Nuclear history was in touch with our feelings and beliefs so thank you for this unusual approach.

This is just a book. What do you plan to do about all the anger, passion, & confusion it only hints at.

This [*visit to the museum*] will help me and my sister at school.

*A lifesize statue of General Leslie Grove at the Bradbury Science Museum.*

*A lifesize statue of Dr. J. Robert Oppenheimer at the Bradbury Science Museum.*

# POINT AND COUNTERPOINT

*This chapter contains quotes which prompted others to respond directly to that quote and sometimes there is a third and fourth comment.*

*Someone from Michigan wrote the following comment:*

Why is it so important that we find ways to kill each other?

*To which someone else responded:*

So we all may survive!

*Point:*

Thank you! Didn't expect to see the truth in this museum.

*And Counterpoint:*

Give me a break!

*Point:*

Having visited Hiroshima, its museum and Peace Park, three weeks ago, this wall is not large enough to present the "other story".

*And counterpoint:*

Did the Hiroshima museum have a wall dedicated to the true proposition that nuclear weapons kept the peace?

*Someone made the point:*

Americans, thank God, are still free to choose— . . .

Thank you!

*To which someone else added:*

AMEN!

*And someone else further added:*

Christians continue to "thank" their god for man's inhumanity to man.
*P.T.L.*
*[Said sarcastically]*

*Someone else felt compelled to scribble all over the page containing this material. Obviously this person was not a pacifist.*


*An American veteran of World War II wrote the simple sentiment:*

Thank you for saving my life.
PVT.
32D INF. DIV.
1945

*To which a person who identified himself as Japanese responded:*

Me too  3 children  7 grand children   Pilot 5th Air Force 1945


*A humorist wrote:*

Did Clinton come here?

*Not to be undone, another humorist responded:*

I hope that Clinton came here.

*Either a humorist or a person with religious convictions wrote:*

Smile Jesus Loves you!

*To which a cynic wrote:*

Big deal. Why doesn't he send me a million bucks if he loves me so much?

*And a pessimist and cynic wrote:*

What can one say? Will mankind solve our problems—I think not!!

*To which an optimist responded:*

Yes, mankind can solve its problems. It always has.

*In the following sequence, which is one of my favorites, a woman from Denver wrote:*

I now know what a missile cruise looks like!

*To which her husband responded:*

My wife does not know what she is talking about. (This should read cruise missile.)

*To which the wife responded:*

But at least I'm in medical school and I will someday save lives!

*The following appears to be a poem. I do not know the origin of this poem. The person who wrote it in the ledger could very well be the author. Then again, it may well be a classic. It would seem that this item belongs in the "PROFOUND" chapter for it does indeed appear quite profound. However, there seemed to be so much reaction to this material with point and counterpoint that I have chosen to place it here.*

*The following poem appeared. I have tried to represent it in the same stanza form that it was written.*

"I come and stand at
every door but no one hears my
silent tread
I knock and yet remain unseen
for I am dead for I am dead

I'm only 7 altho I died at
Hiroshima long ago
I'm 7 now as I was then
When children die they do not grow.

My hair was scorched by swirling flame
My eyes grew dim, my eyes grew blind
death came & turned my bones to dust & that was
scattered by the wind.

All that I ask is that for Peace
We fight today we fight today
So that the children of this world may
live & grow & laugh & play."

*Apparently the following is a commentary by the person who presented the prior poem. The handwriting appeared to be the same.*

We should apologize to <u>Japan</u> for using A-Bombs—There is power in an apology. Not saying we are right or wrong—but we are sorry. —

*And then a counterpoint to the above:*

Note that Japan has <u>never</u> apologized for its role in WW II—Not to China, not for Pearl Harbor, not for Korean "comfort women" . . .

*And another counterpoint to the previous:*

Remember Pearl Harbor

*And counterpoint to the counter-point:*

Speak for yourself . . . All's fair in love & <u>war</u>!

*The following commentary was on the same page as the prior material and appeared to be a direct response to the other comments on the page.*

Has it occurred to anyone that having diffused the bombs over Hiroshima and Nagasaki—no one else has <u>dared</u> to try it again?—And—having brought the Japanese war lords to defeat— (While saving the lives of countless allied forces in the Pacific)—The world learned a severe lesson!

Wife of Navy Man who worked
on invasion maps of Japan.

*The following sequence brought out some very strong emotions.*

Admittedly, war is not the answer to man's differences but it was not we who invaded Poland, and it was not we who bombed Pearl Harbor. Better 210,000 Japanese than my father or his buddies.

Son of WW II veteran

P.S. Maybe if we had used the bomb against North Korea, there wouldn't have been a Vietnam.

*And counterpoint:*

This is sick!!

[*Apparent reference to prior quote about North Korea.*]

*And counterpoint to counterpoint:*

I'm glad that not all visitors think like that one.

a European

*Point:*

Give LANL scientists space to rebut the peacenik propaganda wall.

*Counterpoint:*

You have the entire museum to do that!

*And counterpoint:*

So let the dog [*watchDOG—meaning LASG*] group build their own!


*Point:*

May we never forget Hiroshima & Nagasaki!

*And Counterpoint:*

Nor Pearl Harbor!


*Point:*

Let's make all forms of destruction tomorrow's antiques! Let's progress not regress.

Yea for solar
power!!

*And Counterpoint:*

Boo-Hiss
Let's turn your lights out first!!
Then you'll see nukes are good.

*A plaintive plea!*

> Can't we all just get along?
> [*There was a drawing of hands shaking here.*]

*And a very depressing response!*

> NO!

*A cynic expressed:*

> The only interest of this museum is, to glorify nuclear weapons and energy I believe. (A German)

*To which a historical moralist responded:*

> Germany has no monopoly on peace & morality!! On the merits may Americans show your concern.

*And a little bit of repartee humor:*

> Ban the bomb!

*To which someone retorted sarcastically:*

> Get a life.

*One could easily get into an endless debate with point and counterpoint of the following material.*

The many truly enthusiastic and uncritical comments in this book reveal an attitude which, if combined with all the nuclear weapons in this country, is as threatening as the weapons themselves!

Germany

*And counterpoint:*

And before that they bashed each other with clubs—so what's your point?

*And counterpoint to counterpoint:*

How many people does a club kill? How many people does a bomb kill?

*A person with quite strong opinions wrote:*

I found that this museum glorified war, destruction, and nuclear bombs, rather than the good that it could do. The exhibits focus on the power of the bomb rather than the effects which it had on human beings. One bomb wiped out thousands of people. Is this humane? The nuclear bombs did one side. If we unleash it upon ourselves, we are opening another "Pandora's Box". For the future's sake—PREVENT THIS FROM HAPPENING.

*To which someone else felt challenged to make the following counterpoint:*

Did you see all the exhibits in the museum, or limit yourself to one topic?!?

*This quote has so much to say in a short commentary I felt compelled to duplicate it in the section on PROFOUND comments.*

To stand at ground zero at Nagasaki where the flowers bloom and the shards of those who died are underfoot, then to come to Los Alamos and see the source of the awesome power is a real Alpha and Omega.

*Again there are always those who wish to present another side.*

Maybe you would understand better if you were a Caucasian resident of Singapore, Hong Kong, Shanghai, Manilla or the Dutch East Indies in '42—wake up and smell the roses—you're here today because of the bomb!

*The rhetorical question was posited:*

How about statistics on rates of cancer, suicide, alcoholism, domestic abuse, etc. among the people in Los Alamos?

*So someone provided an answer to the prior question:*

Actually, among the residents of Los Alamos there has been no significant increase in the death rate of cancer. Los Alamos does have however the highest rate of Ph.D's per capita than anywhere in the U.S. plus a huge percentage of high school graduates who go on to college. So give me a break about how bad it must be to live here. I grew up here and consider myself more open minded well traveled and healthy than a lot of people who grew up in "normal" communities elsewhere.—A Los Alamos native.

*Here we have a British view of history:*

Most museum's exhibits do not reflect the impartial view necessarily to truly educate with an open mind. This is to justify the past or the future of Nuclear research. Some of the mindless stupidity expressed in this book [*the ledger*] is testimony to the American viewpoint that anything they do can never ultimately be wrong. Remember the war was all but over when your generals decided to truly test the bomb in Japan. If Hiroshima was "necessary", what was Nagasaki?

An Englishman

*And a different American view:*

If you hadn't disarmed yourselves into impotence after World War I there might not have been a world war II. By 1941 England had lost the war—we, with weaponry that you swear at, had to bail you out. I am very sick of Europeans and their holier than thou attitude—telling Americans how to run our lives and our past evils—like they have so much to be proud of!

*Many of the so-called following "counterpoints" are not counterpoints at all but rather strong agreement with previous comments. This is true with respect to the following sequence.*

Opinions on nuclear research and development are fine, but how many of those who have inscribed their fiery statements in this ledger are <u>doing something about</u> what they view as the problem?

—Signed—the voice<br>of reason

P.S. Be wary of hypocrites!

*And agreement:*

This is the best message in the whole book!

*The following is an interesting quote. It is obviously a play on the anti gun control advocate's quote that "Guns don't kill people. People kill people." The interesting thing is that this quote is from an Australian and NOT an American.*

*Point:*

> Bombs don't kill people, people kill people.

> Australia

*Counterpoint:*

> But people drop bombs!!

*And agreement:*

> Good call.

*The following commentary really brought out point and counterpoint and counterpoint after counterpoint. It is apparent that all of these comments are interrelated because of the way they appeared on the page in the ledger but it is not clear in every case which comment was being referred to in each counterpoint.*

*Point:*

> This [*the Wall*] is an outrageous display unless you display what the Japanese empire did 1) rape of Nanking 2) attack on Pearl Harbor when we were not at war 3) the Bataan death march—many New Mexican soldiers.

*Counterpoint:*

> The display is not about atrocities done by governments so much as our capability to destroy so completely with such distance that it seems more like a movie than a reality.

19

*And here a Dutch citizen expresses a viewpoint:*

> It is a pity that Americans seem to try to solve their problems in a <u>technical</u> way: fights for symptoms instead of facing the cures. E.G. the environment problems, the decadent amount of energy the average U.S. citizen needs. It seems that you like to solve the problems of others instead of making a step backward <u>yourself</u>. Where is your responsibility or [*are*] you opportunists who are afraid of change?

Dutch citizen

*And some agreement:*

> <u>Read this one!!</u>

*This comment was definitely a reference to prior comments but it is not clear who or what is being referred to. It is probably referencing the anti-American sentiment.*

> Jackass.

*And a little more chauvinism:*

> Why do you come to our country?

*And even more:*

> An egg-headed liberal.

*With some counterpoints to the previous remarks:*

> An anonymous American who I am embarrassed to share citizenship.

*And some more counterpoint:*

> With the increasing trust in technology to solve our problems - <u>and not</u> ideas - has come a troubling incapacity to handle self-criticism. Perhaps when we are willing and able to deal with criticism, and those who lodge them, with more than "egg-headed liberal", perhaps then we can use the technology we have created in responsible ways.

# FUNNY, HUMOROUS, CUTE, CLEVER

*There has apparently been a host of would-be comedians visiting the Bradbury museum. Some of the quotes which might have appeared here are in Point and Counterpoint and perhaps some other sections as well.*

*One humorist wrote:*

Kmart HAS A <u>sale</u> on Thermo-Nuc. warheads (Isle 12) 1 per customer.

*This is one of my absolute favorites. Some quite obvious sarcasm is intended in the following quote:*

"Eye licked thiss musam andy eye wont too bee aye partt of itt won uv theez dais. Whow due eye rejistir four thiss cind ov job. If infomatun pleeze cal me Numbre—G#!-"&@i

thanches

[*Translation*]—"I liked this museum and I want to be a part of it one of these days. How do I register for this kind of job. If [*you have*] information, please call me. —Telephone—???-????—thanks"

*To which someone who apparently missed the sarcasm and the intended humor responded:*

And what about your spelling?

*A little tongue in cheek humor.*

It was fun. This place is too small.

God

*Someone really has it in for someone named Davis. I'm glad I'm not Davis:*

Davis molests small children.

Davis is into beastiality.

Davis is a phlegm pie!

*My spell checker indicates that horrific is not a word. However, I think that the writer had intended a double meaning.*

I thought it (the museum at large) was horrific.

*This one has got my curiosity. Is it entirely a fictitious piece of humor or was there such a test with cockroaches? The implication is that there was such a test on July 18, 1993 to July 25, 1993.*

Don't <u>fear</u> the radiation; EAT the plutonium—mutate and evolve like we did.

>Cockroach #5,
>910, 109, 673
>Master Sergeant
>Time Travel Test #3
>7-18-25 1993

*Some school kid was glad to be here.*

Thanks for inviting us—we don't have to go to school.

*The following standard appeared.*

Make love not war!

*To which someone who might describe himself (I assume it is a he—women do not usually think this way) as a militaristic lover, replied:*

Make love and war.

The following quote had me intrigued. It was on the first page of the first ledger. I suspect that what it means is that the pen provided for the public was a pretty good pen. I suspect that the writer might have confiscated said pen.

**What a Pen!**

Someone went to a lot of effort to produce the following artwork and humourous commentary.

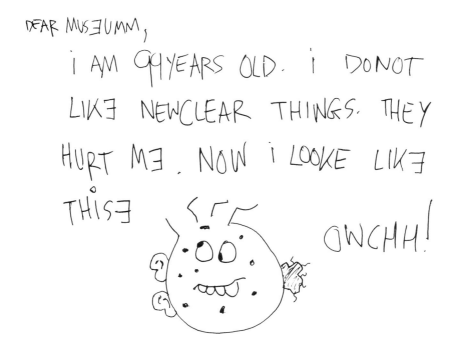

# THE CURIOUS,
# IRRELEVANT, IMPERTINENT, OBSCURE

*The following quotes are either irrelevant, impertinent or obscure. They provoke less of a chuckle and more of a scratching of one's head and a furrow in one's brow. For some of these quotes it is hard to understand why someone wrote what they did. Other quotes seem to contradict themselves. Others seem to make no sense at all.*

Drag The Pass For View Into The Thousand Eyed Present.

R.W. Emerson

The atomic bomb was pretty cool! It's very interesting!

I love Jeff!

Although your museum advocates weapons of destruction and chaos, which are both <u>sure</u> to be the downfall of humanity I enjoyed it very much. Thank you.

*The following was in a child's handwriting.*

P.S. It was a fun place.

*To which another child responded:*

It was not a fun place, thank you. Person who is not happy.

25

*Someone wrote:*

I love all my friends.
Rebecca

*To which someone commented:*

<u>Homo</u>


*More really curious comments.*

I went to sleep during the film, and the only reason why we came because it was on the way out!

Viva the mountainbike!!! (Sweden)

John Lennon is an old fart, who shouldn't have gone solo! Ringo RULES!

It was cool to see the home of the Nuclear Bomb. See ya

(Wisconsin, Moo Country)

Science is a fools endeavor. We are pushing to become Gods, finding only apocalypse. I encourage the testing and use of Nuclear weapons, we've been like a virus to this planet, it's time for us to leave.

I want to see a real atomic explosion.

Our country reeks of trees
Our Yaks are really large and
Smell like rotting beef carcuses
—Royal Canadian Kilted Yaksmen

*The following comment is interesting. It is fairly obvious that President Clinton did not present this comment. However, it is not clear who provided the addition of "not" and did the "not" appear with the signature or before?*

>        not
>         V
> The world is cool.
>         Bill Clinton

I liked the elephants best.
The hippo's were cute too!

This whole exhibit reminds me of a comment Hans-Jorgen Weierstraub made—A person with chicken coops has no need for a plumber.

"In the last days—there will be wars, and rumors of wars, and men fainting for fear of what is to come —" —in other words, business as usual.

*This set of comments seemed to have come from a related group of school children.*

This museum is Boring

I think I LIKE THIS PLACE

This isn't McDonalds

*And written in all bold letters:*

IF IT'S NOT LOVE, THEN IT'S THE BOMB THAT WILL BRING US TOGETHER . . .
               Manchester, England
*[Really???]*

Peace is louder than Bombs.

*I think that "this station" in the following comment refers to the location of the "Alternative Perspectives" wall which invites the visitor to write their comments.*

I don't understand this station here. The directions confuse me very much. But, I think nuclear energy is bad. It kills people. We need to end this war.

[*I wonder which war they are referring to.*]

*Some people might consider the following quote quite profound. I find it quite curious.*

I think nuclear energy and weapons are good. How <u>else</u> can we make the world's countries unite?

*The following comment is presented exactly as it was written with the exception that the name was changed. What strikes me is that this quote was written by someone who belonged to a Nuclear Science Club but they can't spell Museum nor Nuclear. Heaven help us with future scientists like this.*

Best Meusem

John Doe

Nucla Science Club!

*And what the heck does this mean????*

To be strongly attached to one end of the dichotomy is to ensure the continuing existence & strength of the other end.

*However, someone who seems to think that they understand the message, wrote:*

I agree wholeheartedly

*I have tried to present the following entry as closely identical to the original as possible. There is a complete message here but I am not sure what it is. The author/artist used 1/2 a page for the entry.*

STRENGTH

PLUS =                    SECURITY

RESPONSIBILITY


POWER
                          HITLER
PLUS =                    HIROHITO
                          STALIN
IGNORANCE                 MUSSOLINI


LOVE
HATE
PEACE
WAR

*I believe that the following is in reference to the "Alternative Perspectives" exhibit. The "Alternative Perspectives" is pretty clear what it is about to most viewers. That is why I find this entry most curious.*

WHAT IS THE EXHIBIT ABOUT?

*Again the following entry is being represented as close as possible to the original. The curious thing about this entry is that someone had crossed out "GOD" in the entry and scribbled in "Buddha". Someone else then chose to add a bit of sarcasm with the "ya right" entry and the arrows.*

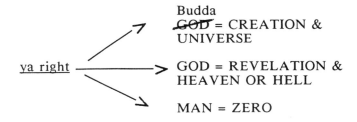

Budda
~~GOD~~ = CREATION & UNIVERSE

<u>ya right</u>

GOD = REVELATION & HEAVEN OR HELL

MAN = ZERO

*The person responsible for the following inscription put it in quotes implying that it is from some other source. Perhaps it is.*

"In the deep dark night of the soul it is always 3 o'clock in the morning,."

*Some people have different agendas.*

I liked the movie—especially the boys.

*And some views are simplistic but profound.*

Read "The Butter Battle" by Dr. Seuss—the answers to this chaos lie in the simplicity of nature.

May peace prevail
May peace someday prevail

*The following comment was written in Japanese. My translator, a native of Japan and a student at the University of New Mexico, wrote the following comment to me:*

*(I'm sure this one sounds a little strange. It sounded strange even in Japanese.)*

科学はすごい。ここは科学博物館で、戦争には関係ない。
戦争のことについてはあまりふれられていけないいけど、
これでいいのかなあと思う。
ここに来て私はとても日本人だなあと思った。
アメリカ人にはなれないんだなあやっぱり。
3月10日(水) 1994年

[*Translation*]

Science is amazing. Since this is a science museum, it has nothing to do with wars. They rarely mention the wars, and I wonder if it is all right to do this. (Not to mention the wars.) I came to find that I am very Japanese. I can't be an American, after all.

Wednesday,
March 10th, 1994

*The following comment was written in German. It is difficult to understand the intended message. The comment was signed as if it is a direct quote of Richard Wagner, presumbably the German composer. "Richard Wagner" was followed by the actual name of the person who entered the material. It is also curious that the author of the comment indicates that he is from Santa Fe High School. Most curious!!!*

Ich weiß nicht wo
ich bin oder warum. Ich
bin nur hier. Wir sind
glücklich und zufrieden, aber
nicht so falsch. Das tut mir
leid. Ich weiß nicht was ich
schreibe. Mein Deutsch ist
nicht so gut, eh? Ich bin
nur ein Deutsch 3 Schüler aus
Santa Fe Oberschule
　　　　　　Richard
　　　　　　Wagner

[*Translation*]

I know not where I am or why. I am only here. We are happy and satisfied, but not so false. I'm sorry. I don't know what I'm writing. My German is not so good, is it? I am only a 3rd year high school student from Santa Fe HS.

Richard Wagner
Germany


What the hell are you guys going to do with your <u>nuclear waste</u> and radioactive byproducts that are so harmful for thousands and thousands of years? Bury them and hope your children will know what to do?

New Zealand

P.S. The "hot, dry rock" idea is a good one, good luck.!!

P.P.S. Most of the South Pacific is grateful to the American GIs who sacrificed so much during World War II.

# THE PROFOUND,
# ARTICULATE, THOUGHT PROVOKING

*I selected the following comments for this section because they seemed to be more thought provoking than anything else. Some will appear to be pro-nuclear and some anti-nuclear but there is a thread of deep thought to all of them.*

*I have elected not to provide any running commentary for this section with the exception of some foreign text. I believe that most of the comments speak for themselves.*

One of the major arguments I hear against nuclear weapons is their cause of extensive collateral damage. In Nagasaki & Hiroshima combined, I believe about 180,000 people died (pretty much all civilians) . . . When a life is lost to Nuclear weapons, people seem to count that as a more tragic, criminal loss than when conventional tools of death are used." . . .
"But too often the question 'Is war acceptable' is confused with the question 'What kind of war is acceptable' and this nefariously clouds the issue."

I am stuck with what to say. I do not believe in war, or finding new more efficient ways of killing people—but my family on both sides, worked here, worked on the bombs. What does that make me?
  \* Another thought
   Can anything or one be <u>all</u> "Good" or <u>all</u> "Bad"?

I love the alternative exhibit. It is the only human, moral, element in a space so technological that death is merely an abstraction . . . even life seems an abstraction.

I guess the bomb was inevitable. Still I'd hate to be one of those scientists . . .

It is unfortunate that technology has brought the destruction of so many lives. However, it should not be forgotten that the bomb was released in a war situation. War takes away choices that we can make in peace time.

*The following is Chinese text:*

我是一位中国人到这来探讨。来到此馆
给我很大给示。看见我到到科研者的伟
大为你们让人们尊敬。我到到美国二伟大
视你们认意心立去足囬。

我这一生不能的科研囬神入足囬 很遗
憾憾。我也如果我有了你一定到这么事
对二为美囬、为人美科学极度献.

我也也也也我二全命对二为此 做奉献
哪怕一炎儿。

谢谢 你们 谢谢 美囬科学引以为荣. 谢在
本馆的有人员. 谢谢 美囬政府 给你们有机
机会。

—— 一个普通中囗人 和他和他儿子 一记事。

荻山石. 此京 1994. 6.

儿子 荻峰 住美州

[*Translation*]

I am a Chinese. I travel here. After I visited this museum,
I found that how great scientist are and why people
respect them. I also understood why the United States is
great and why Americans love their country.

I regret that I cannot work in the science field in my life.
If my descendants have opportunities to work here, I wish
they could make big contributions to Americans, and to
whole people in the world.

I wish I will be able to make some contributions to
mankind in my remaining life.
Thank you. I thank all American scientists. Thank people
who are working in this museum. Thank the government
of the United States for giving me an opportunity to visit
here.

> [*Signed*] A common
> citizen of China and
> my son.
> Beijin & Connecticut
> June 1994

*The following is written in Greek:*

Είμαι ένα πολύ μικρό παιδί απο την Ελλάδα
σας παρακαλώ ΟΧΙ! πυρηνικά ότι πόλεμο
ΕΙΡΗΝΗ ΕΙΡΗΝΗ ΑΓΑΠΗ

Είμαστε όλοι αδέλφια

[*Translation*]     Athens - Greece

I am a very small child from Greece, please, I beg of you, no
nuclear weapons or other items of war.

Peace peace peace

We are all brothers

Athens—Greece

*The following is one of many comments written in German:*

Da ich von Deutschland ein
falls es mir schwer zu glauben was dieser
Staat für schaden in der Welt verursacht hat.
Ich Bin 13 Jahre alt, aber finde es nicht
gut, das andere denken, nur weil ich von
Deutschland bin muss ich jetzt auch ân
Nazi sein. Danke, das ich meine
Gedanken hier niederschreiben durfte.

[*Translation*]

As I am from Germany, it is hard for me to believe what harm in the world this country has caused. I am 13 yrs. old, but find it not good that others think, merely because I am from Germany, that I must be a Nazi. Thank you for allowing me to express my thoughts here.

I believe the destruction of so many innocent lives was horrible. However, I have never experienced the horror of war and I am in no position to judge either the scientists or soldiers involved with the bomb. Every day I benefit from the freedom others fought for! Thanks!!

To stand at ground zero at Nagasaki where the flowers bloom and the shards of those who died are underfoot, then to come to Los Alamos and see the source of the awesome power is a real Alpha and Omega.

Once asked, a question can never be forgotten. As long as humans have existed, someone has asked "what if?" Knowledge is neither good nor bad—it is the use of such knowledge which determines its goodness! For the sake of life as we know it, it is time to concentrate on the ethics of knowledge as well as the acquisition thereof.

Even though I am only in the 8th grade I find this quite confusing yet interesting. I feel like I have just opened a new book and learned something very interesting about the history of the U.S. and the world.

War is terrible. Atomic weapons are efficient. Philip Morrison has it right. Hamburg, Tokyo, Dredsen & Leipzig were destroyed by continuous day & night bombing over many days. Casualties were in the thousands—as much as Hiroshima and Nagasaki. But thousand plane raids/day involving tens of thousands of servicemen. The problem is war, not the means of waging it.

I can respect a pacifism which says, "Do your worst—kill my defenseless children, kill me—I will not voluntarily harm another human being." I can also respect a stance which says, "I will never initiate aggression but if I see you hurting & torturing & murdering others, especially those whom I am responsible for (my children, my compatriots, etc.) I will stop you with all necessary force." Defense is a sad necessity unless one is brave enough to choose death/degradation not only for oneself but for one's family and fellow-citizens . . .

This ["The Wall"] is the most thought provoking, challenging part of the museum. We all need to question our beliefs and values every so often.

I visited Hiroshima and was sad. Los Alamos & the display & movie makes me afraid, very afraid.

I really enjoyed this museum. It brought a lot of thoughts into my head though. I remember once I read somewhere that when scientist & engineers make things, they always say, "we could, we could". But no one stopped to think of the should.

One has to wonder reading history, if the bomb didn't finally make men realize that war must end. Have we ever had so long a period of peace as end of Vietnam—'72 to today?

Much to my surprise and amazement I recognized my friend's handwriting describing the elements of a nuclear reactor as a part of the omega west reactor display, and am reminded of how we all came full circle in our own individual ways, eventually, and how each of us has our own part to play in the history and destination of our country and our world.

It all makes you stop and think, doesn't it?

Who are we to decide the morality of any of this technology? Human beings are but half-a-blink-of-an-eye in the life of this earth. We will come and we will go—and if any one of us thinks technology will change that—the laugh's on them. Stay informed.

Very interesting museum—lots to learn or choosing not to.

(Britain)

With the breakup of the USSR & the Eastern Block there is <u>absolutely</u> no need for this situation to continue. Your exhibit is very deceptive. Only here and there does one get a true picture, What about McCarthyism? What about the disgraceful treatment of Oppenheimer? And the execution of the Rosenbergs will remain a [ ]. And what about today's problem of contamination, and why not support Pres. Clinton's moratorium on testing. He deserves much more support.

Something that exists <u>can never</u> be wholly forgotten nor destroyed.

Healthy disagreement is good, but some people seem to start mindlessly ranking on the town and the museum. This book <u>is for healthy disagreements</u>. Think, and for god's sake, know what you're talking about. All of the exhibits here are factual and relatively objective. Please, if you're going to write, <u>do the same</u>!!

If peace is defined as the absence of war, then we have enjoyed more peace since the development of nuclear weapons. But peace is <u>not</u> the absence of war. War is the absence of peace. Peace is well being, happiness, comfort—peace of mind. We have not been at peace since 1945. No weapon, no matter how terrible, will end all wars. Wars will end when every human being decides that peaceful relations with his fellow humans are preferable to war. Nuclear weapons are a pain, and attempts to justify them is detrimental rationalizations, wrong headed at best and dangerous at worst.

Revisionism is one of the sins of mankind!

It is very easy to speak of the evils engaging in war when you are not engaged in one.

The photos of the nuclear explosions are incredibly beautiful. The photos of the burned bodies are incredibly horrifying. Both are awe inspiring, astonishing. The Yin & the Yang.

Research into all avenues of science is necessary. However, the wisdom and compassion that must always be to temper <u>development</u> of research is the most necessary part of modern science. Ignorance is not bliss, but rather a crime. Decisions as to the fate of <u>all</u> research, not just weapons, should be made by many common people. That all people should be so informed is an unrealistic hope, but all should strive to learn. Such decisions should not be confined (on the knowledge that allows them to be made) to the powers that be. I have enjoyed both sides of the discussion presented. Opinions are necessary.

Thank you for completing the story. The accomplishments of LANL scientists during WW II will remain the most significant fact of our country—and the most painful dilemma of our conscience.

I hope that the new generation of young scientists will bring a sense of vulnerability of our species and fragility of the earth to our work. It's difficult, though. During our graduate training we are implicitly taught that the greatest scientific endeavors are those which are most divorced from human considerations. When we struggle against this attitude we are diminished in the eyes of our mentors.

Perhaps it is human destiny to become a species capable of destroying everything. There is no answer. We can't all be nice to each other. We have to just accept our hate because there's nothing we can do about it now. [age 17]

[EDITORIAL NOTE—IT IS TRULY SAD TO OBSERVE SUCH PESSIMISM, ESPECIALLY FROM A 17 YEAR OLD.]

Nuclear energy can kill (bombs) & save (nuclear medicine) individual people—our neighbors, ourselves. What is most needed in the U.S. is an informed public that both of these are the consequences of the technology developed at Los Alamos in the past & in today. On that note, I'd like to congratulate this museum for its refusal to dilute technological principles in these displays. I hope that all who visit will come away better informed (scientifically) & with an interest to study further the issues.

There is, as of today, the simple fact that World War III has not occurred. We cannot know whether Los Alamos is responsible for this shaky but enjoyable peace. Certainly we can fear that had others developed the bomb our freedom and peace would exist only in history.

So many questions, not enough answers.
                    Child age 11

I wish there were a simpler solution.

                    Signed, Peace and safety.

When you see children fight about something how do you feel? They fight about silly things. We are all children.

As a sister of a person who is currently studying nuclear physics, I know its not his intention to harm the world but help. While much is known, so much more is unknown. I don't believe the quest for knowledge can be stopped so scientists will undoubtedly discover more. God grant them wisdom.

Ironically, although nuclear weapons are the most lethal weapons ever built, few people realize that in the their 50 years history they have been used in war only twice and that resulted in the deaths of a number of people that shrinks to insignificance in comparison to all those who have died in war by guns.

I just find it interesting that Henry Adams predicted, in 1862 or thereabouts that, in his opinion, scientists would soon enable the human race to destroy themselves, as well as all life on the planet.

50 years later and we're finally getting a genuine discussion of alternative views at LANL Science Lab—that's democracy, thought belated!

The contents of the 20 minutes lasting movie about the Manhattan Project being an interesting historic document, it nevertheless occurs to us Europeans, that the way in which things are presented is still typical "American-Coco-Cola, Walt Disney-like." As if you people always have to ease your minds with syrup-like pictures like Crucifixes praying good Christians (to start a film about the Atomic bomb) and technological innovations (to end it). Why not stick to the true story? What about the things your government did to J. Robert Oppenheimer after the war?

Professor of Physics
—Belgium

As one who was born, have lived under, and escaped communism, I fully endorse the effort to maintain a strong defense. I am very disturbed by many comments in this book which display a shocking naivety of the rest of the world. It seems that many Americans have extended their culture-ethnocentricity to the extreme that all others share their values. I can assure you they do not—and they wish you harm. Preparedness is not a crime against humanity.

Sergei [*A Russian*]

I believe we need to concentrate on cleaning our house more than harming others. I have seen that the awareness of the public has led us in the right direction. I hope that our 10 x great grand [*meaning ten generations hence*] kids can thank our wisdom and not curse our sins.

You're damned if you do and damned if you don't! Who knows the answer?

# PRO-NUCLEAR,
# ANTI-NUCLEAR, POLITICAL, NEUTRAL

*The following quotes are all directed at nuclear energy, nuclear research, the atomic bomb or the politics of any of these. I considered making separate chapters for each of the types presented here but decided to intermix the comments. I also considered including a running commentary but the material did not lend itself to inclusion of my unbiased commentary. The comments in this chapter speak for themselves. The readers can decide for themselves whether a sentiment is pro-nuclear, anti-nuclear or otherwise.*

. . . Nuclear is not a bad word—its not the concept of the thing but how you use it and for what purposes—we have lived a long time with nuclear weapons.


It's all too complicated for one to grasp. Reactions & how the continued ultimate cost advantages of nuclear electricity when accidents & waste disposal are factored in.


As one who would not be here today if it were not for the <u>bomb</u>, I was in a POW camp about 40 miles from Nagasaki as slave labor in a coal mine. If Japan was invaded we would all be killed. Horrible as it was as I flew over Nagasaki on the way out all I could think of how thankful it was and the killing would stop.

Survivor of Bataan &<br>Corregidor

"Think about this—we stop nuclear research and all the good & positive aspects of it die. . . . There can be a balance and should be. . . . Just stop for a moment and realize that there is room for the Nuclear Age . . .

How about we go back to the horse and buggy days for 3 yrs. then maybe the hippies and other such idiots will see the light!

The biggest Question raised by L.A. research is one of Ethics. Many of the Scientists who worked on the project were not there to create some mega war-machine, merely to discover more about the world around them. Any abuse of their research is purely the fault of the gov't's of the world. The scientists should not be blamed.

I feel the maintenance of a strong military deterrent is essential to assuring our way of life.

I would have our nation do it again to protect our freedom.

If in 1945 our scientists could see into the future . . . would they have decided to continue on with "Atomic Power", or dismantle everything so that no nuclear world problems would ever exist?

The answer is obvious.

" . . . What about the benefits of all the nuclear research in the life sciences arena?

Without the defense that these nuclear weapons maintain, we might not be here to view this museum. I support the work done here 100%.


As an American I have very mixed feelings about the bomb! Is there an answer? I'm not sure.


## Remember

It is only because the U.S. has the capabilities developed at LANL that those who espouse the shrill, propaganda style messages on the "Alternative Perspectives" wall have the freedom to express their view.


Thank you for your dedication to speaking the truth in this National Monument to denial, and weapons addiction.


Using these weapons is like spending our children's future.

*The following is German text:*

Wir sind eine kleine Gruppe Touristen aus Deutschland. Leider haben wir nicht alle gegebenen Informationen verstehen können. Was uns aber unverständlich ist, wie man so eine schreckliche Waffe, wie die Atombombe, derart glorifizieren kann.

[*Translation*]

We are a small group of tourists from Germany. Unfortunately we were unable to understand all of the available information. What is however incomprehensible is how such an awful weapon like the atom bomb can be glorified in such a way.

Germany

To all who stand before this book—Did you come here today in your car bought with money you earned in the U.S. doing the job you chose? Will you have enough to eat tonight? Are you free to express your opinion—no matter how radical? That freedom has a price. If you don't believe it, it's time for a world tour at your free library for a reality check!

If the bomb were not developed—sure, the war would have ended anyway. But we would have lost—and the bomb would eventually be made elsewhere. I'm glad we made it first.

Debate is always good—but lets hear both sides—the Lab doesn't just produce N. Weapons and Nuclear Power could save the world and environment.

There aren't enough pages in this book to list all of the United States servicemen who survived WW II as a result of the use of "nuclear things". Even our enemy has expressed thanks for the summary conclusion of that conflict resulting from use of "nuclear things." May God enlighten your understanding nature!

Not a judgement, just more data: Recently declassified documents show that Japan, not Germany, was the other contender in the race to build an atomic bomb. They were less than a year away from an independently researched, developed, and successfully built bomb at the time of the Hiroshima drop. And yes, they would certainly not hesitate to use it!

*The following is German text:*

Wir finden es erschreckend wie positiv hier die Atomwaffentechnik dargestellt wird. Die Folgen der Abwürfe über Japan und der Atombomben- versuche haben zu wenig Raum.
Wir sind erschreckt über die Erkenntnis mit unserer Meinung alleine dazu stehen.

GERMANY

[*Translation*]

We find it terrifying how positively the atom bomb is presented. The consequences of the bombing of Japan and the research/experimentation concerning the atom bomb are given too little place. We are worried at finding ourselves alone in our opinion.

Germany

If there had not been a Pearl Harbor there would not have been a Hiroshima.

Let us not forget the lessons of history and the folly of total disarmament.


Carbon dioxide, sulphur oxide, dust, clearing rain forests are slowly poisoning our earth. If we want to use energy at these levels the clean nuclear power will be essential. Let the search for fission power continue, in the way Los Alamos worked in the 40's! The U.S. uses more energy per capita than any other country in the world. Why not turn down all those air conditioners? In Holland 1/3 of all trees is dead and dying! The best solution is a dramatic reduction of population growth, but unfortunately that's out of our control.

                                        Holland


*The following is written in the Latvian language:*

[*Translation*]

I have seen that about which I have heard for many years. I bow my head on honor of the Los Alamos specialists. I believe that nuclear energy will only serve peace.

                                        Latvia


LANL, thanks for 50 years peace/prosperity in Europe!

                                        (ex-Bosnia)


In September 1945 I called a los Alamos scientist, Dr. Peterson, in response to his call to oppose the May-Johnson Bill which would have put Atomic Energy under the control of the military. We won the battle, but in truth the role of the military in this area has never diminished.

*The following is from South Korea:*

로스 알라모스 방문목적은 원자탄 제조과정을 박물관에서 보려고 했었는데 그밖에 여러가지 다양한 연구, 즉 레이저이동 환경오염대책연구. 건조암반으로부터 에너지, 전기 획득등 평화적 목적의 이용에 대해 감복하는 바 입니다.

Seoul, Korea.

[*Translation*]

I came to visit the museum at Los Alamos because I wanted to see how to process [*make*] nuclear bomb. However I saw many other kinds of studies such as protecting from pollution by using radiant rays, making energy and electricity from dry base rock, and so on. I was impressed because these were for peace.

(Seoul, Korea)

[*It is interesting to note that the author signed this comment as being from Seoul, Korea and NOT Seoul, South Korea.*]

51

*The following is French-Belgium:*

> Montre que la terre possède de très nombreuses capacités ignorées encore à ce jour. Nous ne connaissons encore rien. C'est pourquoi les centres de recherche sont si importants... Important pour que des erreurs telque la bombe atomique ne se reproduira plus
>
> BELGIUM

[*Translation*]

Show that the earth has (very) numerous possibilities still ignored today. We know nothing yet. That is why research centers are so important. Important so that mistakes like the atom bomb will not happen again.

Belgium

*More German text:*

> Nie wieder Forschung für Krieg!!
> Forschung für Erhaltung der Natur, des Menschen und des Lebens!
>
> Germany

[*Translation*]

Never again research for war!! Research for the preservation of nature, of man, and of life.

Germany

52

# DIRECT AND INDIRECT QUOTES

*Sometimes people wrote in the ledgers quotes taken directly from historical figures. Sometimes they would write these quotes and NOT identify the original author although it seemed apparent to me that the quote was from someone else.*

Thomas Jefferson:

"I tremble for my country when I remember that God is just."

"Being prepared for war is the best means of preserving the peace."
                                        George Washington

"WAR IS HELL."
                                        William T. Sherman

"This earth was not given to you to destroy but lent to you by your children."

—This [*the previous quote*] is a really cool quote I had on a shirt. You'd think that all these geniuses from around the world could understand something as simple as that!

WAR IS PEACE
SLAVERY IS FREEDOM
IGNORANCE IS STRENGTH
　　　　　　　—George Orwell
　　　　　　　—1984—

*[1984 is a book written by George Orwell in the 1940s. It is about an oppressive futuristic society in which the apparent illogical statements above are dogma.]*

*I recall seeing the following quotes somewhere else and do believe that they are NOT original comments of the person who inscribed them in the ledger but rather they are direct quotes from some leaders of the past.*

If you would have peace then prepare for war.

"We do not inherent land from our parents. We borrow it from our children."

*Many people mistakenly believe that the following words were penned by Dr. Oppenheimer. Actually, the original author was Bhagavid Gita. It WAS reported that immediately upon the successful explosion of the first atomic bomb, Dr. Oppenheimer said those words. He was merely quoting someone else. It is also mistakenly believed that Dr. Oppenheimer was feeling guilty and engaging in self-accusation. In fact, no further explanation of intent ever was presented by Dr. Oppenheimer.*

"I am become death, the shatterer of worlds."

　　　　　　　—Robert Oppenheimer

I have become death, the shatterer of Worlds!

　　　　　　　Bhagavid Gita

Peace cannot be kept by force . . . But only achieved by understanding.

—A. Einstein

The Swiss are armed to the teeth and they are free.

—Machiavelli

Wer in der Erde grabt
lädt sich Unglück auf.
Spruch eines Indianers
Whc is digging in the earth
is making him unfortunate

—Indian Saying

55

# THE WALL

*Some people were very enthusiastic about "The Wall". Not everyone, however, who observed "The Wall" agreed that it belonged in the museum.*

This is an opening of a dialogue! I'm excited to see the results.

Nice to see a bit of rebuttal to the official reductionism: . . .

Nice to see the other side of the coin!

This exhibit [*alternatives*] is full of inconsistencies and <u>distortions</u>, lies, and paranoia.

Remove "Santa Fe Group" exhibit—it has no place here.

1. Those who produce the *ALTERNATIVE PERSPECTIVES* Are Not Reading Their Own Material. Look at Dr. Bethe's comment made right after WW II—then, the USSR started the arms race and Dr. Bethe was proved wrong. Next, we won the arms race and again Dr. Bethe is almost Correct—which is exactly why today's arsenal has one third of the warheads and one fourth of the megatonage of the peak of the arms race (about 1968).

2. Less damage and death was dealt to Hiroshima and Nagasaki together than was done in one night of fire bombing Tokyo.

3. Never forget these pictures—or the ones of Dresden, London, Leipzig, Warsaw, Kuwait City—that's exactly what happens when people abandon themselves to power, and lust and a disregard for others. If we do not give ourselves up to these, nor allow others to do so, warshot #3 will never be fired.


The Japanese display shouldn't even be here.

# THE SARCASTIC, CAUSTIC

*The following quotes appeared too sarcastic to appear in the chapter with the humorous items and too caustic to appear in any of the serious sections.*

Its not like congress is going to read this [*the ledger*], you know.

[*Perhaps they may read this book.*]

I have an opinion on certain things, but it's no big deal and I'm certain that no one important is going to read this anyway, so why should I put it down.

[*Perhaps someone "important" may read this book.*]

Los Alamos is awesome place to be! Not!

Don't be afraid of Mr. Atom.

What? No photo of the Mitsubishi Steel and Arms works?

[*Now that is classic sarcasm.*]

Can the world not co-operate? Do we need this?

New Zealand

# THE PIOUS, IMPIOUS, IRREVERENT

*The following quotes are either of a religious nature or anti-religious nature. Some people may find some of the comments quite offensive. Then again, people will find some pro-nuclear and some anti-nuclear comments offensive. I wanted to provide equal opportunity for all nature of commentaries, even those which might be offensive to some people. Remember, for every comment which some people might find objectionable, there are a lot of people who will agree with the comment.*

God taught my hands to war (Palmist King David)

So men could be under one God instead of a dictator. Thank God for the plan he gave <u>great</u> minds for the Los Alamos Project.

God almighty gave us atoms & molecules
and their building blocks.
    For good or evil for mankind's use.

It's <u>our choice</u>!
Amen

# SENTIMENTAL AND HISTORICAL

*These quotes generally are from people directly or indirectly involved with the original development of the atomic bomb or were victims of the bomb or had relatives directly or indirectly involved.*

I'm proud of my grandpa—he was called upon to help his country and so he did—he armed "Little Boy"

[*"Little Boy" was the Atomic Bomb dropped on Hiroshima.*]

My uncle Tommy, who was mean as hell, cried when he heard about Hiroshima because he knew the war was over and that he, an infantryman, who'd seen service on Bouganville and the Philippines wouldn't have to go to Japan and be killed there.

I was on a troopship, an infantry assault team, scheduled for the <u>6th wave</u> of the attack on Japan itself, (40 minutes after the first). When the bomb was dropped on Hiroshima—our whole convoy stopped (& milled around for a while). But my life was saved, and tens of thousands of others, and more tens of thousands of Japanese soldiers lives. We live today—sober in the thought.

広島、長崎を繰り返すな。

[*Translation*]

Don't repeat Hiroshima and Nagasaki.

このミュージアムには いろんな ことについての 情報が
あるけど、やっぱり 日本人の 私にとっては "戦争" のことが
一番 印像に 残りました。

世界から 戦争が なくなる ことを、心から 祈ります。
そして、日本と アメリカが より 親しくな ~~━━━━~~ ることを 期待
します。

　　　地球上 すべての人が "平和 (peace)" を 愛すように
　　　　　願いを こめて・・・・

　　　　　　　　　　　　　　　　93　　11月20日 (0)

[*Translation*]

Among all these things in this museum, things about
"war" were the most striking to me as a Japanese.

I hope from the bottom of my heart that wars would
disappear from the world.

And I hope Japan and America would get along better.
Wishing that all the people would love peace . . .

　　　　　　　　　　　Sunday, November
　　　　　　　　　　　20th, 1993

二度とこしたことを(り返したくないと思います。
広島から来れた。

[*Translation*]

I don't want to let the same thing happen twice. I'm from Hiroshima.

原子力が 平和的に 利用されます様!

1993. 8. 13.

(静岡県)

[*Translation*]

I hope the nuclear power will be used peacefully!

1993.8.13
Shizuoka Prefecture

# EPILOGUE

Originally I had not planned on writing an epilogue. As a matter of fact, I had not planned on a prologue either. After I had written most of the material in the *Introduction* I decided to separate some of that material into different sections and I decided to call the new section a *Prologue*. Whether that title is suitable for the material is relatively unimportant. Whether the title of *Epilogue* is suitable for this section is also of little importance. Perhaps I might have appropriately called this section an editorial. I decided that I would use this space to make some personal comments and observations that I have avoided expressing elsewhere.

As I was transcribing some of the comments, I would occasionally be tempted to directly challenge or refute some of those comments. Some of those comments really bothered me as I am certain they have bothered some of you. Faithful to my original objective, I dutifully resisted any temptation to comment directly on any of the sentiments expressed elsewhere. However, I will now offer my comments in this section, in a general and indirect way, on some of the sentiments expressed earlier in this book.

**INACCURATE HISTORICAL OBSERVATIONS**—One of the things I found most bothersome was that some of the statements made wholly inaccurate historical observations. Some of these inaccuracies might seem quite valid to the casual observer since they very often reflect popular misconceptions. Again, sticking to my promise to leave this book open to each reader's interpretation (or misinterpretation), I will not identify those specific comments. However, some people may read such inaccuracies and believe them to be the truth. I strongly urge the reader to engage in some independent research before he or she accepts as absolute truth all of the quotes presented in earlier portions of this book.

**NEGATIVISM**—Another thing I found quite disturbing and troublesome was the extreme negativism, pessimism and defeatism expressed in some of the comments. It seems to me that there is an enormous need as well as justification for optimism in America and in the world. There is more "right" with America than there is "wrong". There is more good to praise in this world than there is bad. There are more benefits accrued as a result of scientific examination than there are negative side affects. And, whatever may be wrong with the American government, the American Constitution or the government that has been created as a product of that constitution, it is still the best in the world. America has more to be proud of than to feel guilty for. So I urge the readers not to be dragged down by some of the negative and pessimistic attitudes found in this book as well as any pessimism they may encounter from other sources. I say to those who have written such negative comments, quit whining and crabbing and fretting. Be happy! Get a life!

**EMOTIONALISM**—Another disturbing characteristic is the emotionalism and lack of objectivity of some of the commentary. The subject of nuclear energy and nuclear bombs will naturally tend to kindle powerful emotions in most people as well as create an environment where objectivity seems to disappear. That, however, is an excuse, not a reason. We must all try to be as objective as we can, even when dealing with controversial subjects such as nuclear energy and atom bombs.

**POLITICAL CORRECTNESS (PC)**—Another thing which disturbs me is that Political Correctness seems to have become an inescapable dimension in our lives. This is indeed unfortunate. We rail at the politicians for being political and yet we practice PC (Political Correctness) ourselves. Isn't this hypocritical? Isn't this irrational? Some of the rebuttals to other people's comments seemed to be based on a desire on the part of the writer to be politically correct. So, my message to you, dear reader, is ALWAYS avoid the Political Correctness trap.

**HISTORICAL PERSPECTIVE**—Last, but not least, is the problem with the lack of historical perspective on the part of some commentators. Hindsight is an amazing thing. With hindsight we can see things so much more clearly. With enough hindsight, I would be the most successful coach in the history of professional football. With hindsight, I could have avoided every accident that shouldn't have happened. With hindsight Pearl Harbor wouldn't have happened. With hindsight, the Titanic disaster would not occur. With hindsight, the Exxon Valdez oil spill would never have happened. Furthermore, Nazi Germany was militarily weak in 1935. If the allies had rebuked Hitler in 1935 (the year Hitler annexed the Saar region and repudiated the Versailles Treaty) and if the allies had taken military action at that time, any engagement would have been over in a week, just like Desert Storm, with few, if any, American casualties. With hindsight, World War II would have been over before it started.

Well, scientists and military and political leaders from yesterday and 30 years ago and 50 years ago and 100 years ago did not have hindsight to assist them in making momentous decisions. They HAD to take risks and they had no way of looking into the future. In so many cases the consequences of their decisions were based on a best guess. (With respect to the first atomic explosion, there was a great deal of skepticism that the first bomb detonated at Trinity Site would work at all. Many of those directly involved expected a complete dud.)

There is a sentiment somewhere which expresses a proposition that we can disagree with the past. One CANNOT disagree with the past. What happened in the past is historical fact. It either happened or it didn't happen. One MAY agree or disagree on the issue of whether an event happened the way it had been reported (such as the Kennedy assassination) but when one accepts the facts of history, one cannot disagree with those facts. Poland WAS invaded, the atomic bomb WAS invented, the attack on Pearl Harbor DID occur, the Holocaust IS a fact of history and an atomic bomb WAS dropped on Hiroshima.

We might wish to disagree with some past decisions others have made. However, in order to do so fairly, we must put the issues in genuine historical perspective. We must try to put ourselves in "their" shoes. This is especially true if it was an event in another era when the parameters and the paradigms were significantly different.

So I urge you to put yourself in the shoes of the decision makers of the time. Become Truman or Roosevelt or Oppenheimer or Eisenhower or Paul Tibbets for a few moments. Are you ABSOLUTELY CERTAIN that YOU would have made decisions which would have been ABSOLUTELY MORALLY, SOCIALLY, AND STRATEGICALLY CORRECT and would have been decisions which would have been judged favorably by future generations?

In the words of a famous would-be politician, "I rest my case."

# ABBREVIATIONS FOUND IN THIS BOOK

LANL—Los Alamos National Laboratory

WW II—World War II

LASG—Los Alamos Study Group

# EXPLANATORY NOTES

**Dr. J. Robert Oppenheimer** had overall responsibility for the scientific aspects of the Manhattan Project.

**General Leslie Groves** was assigned the overall responsibility for the Manhattan Project, especially with respect to military and security issues.

**The Manhattan Project** was the code name for all related aspects of the development of the first nuclear bomb.

**Los Alamos WAS NOT** the exclusive site for Manhattan Project activity. Alamogordo, New Mexico, Oak Ridge, Tennessee, Chicago Stagg Field, Manhattan, New York, the University of California at Berkeley, Hanford, Washington, were some of the other sites where research and development was taking place as well as in England.

**Trinity Site** is the name of the place near Alamogordo, New Mexico, where the first atomic explosion occurred at 5:29:45 a.m., Mountain War Time, on July 16, 1945. The designation "Trinity Project" was the code name chosen by Dr. Oppenheimer for the first atomic explosion and, although there has been much speculation as to why the name was chosen, Dr. Oppenheimer never revealed what he had in mind when he made his choice. Trinity Site is open to the public two days of the year; once in April and once in October. One may actually stand on ground zero where the first atomic explosion occurred on July 16, 1945.

**Bataan and Corrigador** are locales in the Philippines where, early in 1942, American and Philippine forces surrendered to the Japanese army and were forced to undergo severe hardships. The "Bataan Death March" was almost as big a rallying cry for American troops in the Pacific Theater of Operation during World War II as was the remembrance of Pearl Harbor.

**Little Boy and Fat Man** were the names of the bombs used in Hiroshima and Nagasaki respectively.

**Hans-Jorgen Weierstraub** is quoted in this book. My research has not revealed who this person is.

**Albert Einstein** was actually a very key figure in the creation of the Manhattan Project. At the urging of several of his fellow scientists, Dr. Einstein wrote a letter to then President Franklin D. Roosevelt, urging him to provide resources furthering scientific research into nuclear energy. It was Einstein's revelation that Nazi Germany was already working on a "device" which might be of great military significance that resulted in the creation of the Manhattan Project by President Roosevelt.

**Colonel Paul Tibbets** was the pilot of the **Enola Gay** which delivered the atomic bomb to Hiroshima.

**William T. (Tecumseh) Sherman** was an American general with the Union forces. He was responsible for the infamous "Sherman's March To The Sea" in which much destruction took place.

# REFERENCES

For more information you may write to any of the following agencies:

The Bradbury Science Museum
PA-3, Mail Stop C330
Los Alamos, New Mexico 87545
John S. Rhoades, Director

Los Alamos Study Group
212 E. Marcy St.
Santa Fe, New Mexico 87501

Los Alamos National Laboratory
Los Alamos, New Mexico 87545

# BIBLIOGRAPHY—BOOKS

Akizuki, Tatsuichiro. *Nagasaki, Nineteen Forty-Five*. Charles River Books, 1992.

Anderson, Kevin J. *Trinity Paradox*. Bantam Books, 1991.

Anrine, M. *The Great Decision: The Secret History of the Atomic Bomb*. G.P. Putnam & Sons, 1959. (Out of print.)

Badash, Lawrence & Broida, H.P. *Reminiscences of Los Alamos*. Kluwer Academic, 1980.

Bailey, Kathleen C. *Doomsday Weapons in the Hands of Many: The Arms Control Challenge of the '90s*. U. Illinois Press 1991.

Bartimus, Tad & McCartney, Scott. *Trinity's Children: Living Along America's Nuclear Highway*. Harcourt Brace Jovanovich, 1992.

Berne, Stanley & Zekowski, Arlene. *Every Person's Little Book of PLUTONIUM*. Rising Tide Press, 1992.

Beser, Jacob. *Hiroshima & Nagasaki Revisited*. Global Press, 1988.

Bethe, Hans A. *The Road from Los Alamos*. Simon & Schuster, 1991.

Beyer, Don E. *The Manhattan Project: America Makes the First Atomic Bomb*. Watts, Franklin, 1991.

Brodie, Bernard & Brodie, Fawn M. *From Crossbow to H-Bomb*. Indiana U. Press, 1993.

Cantelon, Philip L. & Hewlett, Richard G. & Williams, Robert C. *The American Atom*. U. Pennsylvania Press, 1992.

Carmichael, Virginia. *Framing History: The Rosenberg Story and the Cold War*. U. Minnesota Press, 1992.

Childs, Herbert. *An American Genius: The Life of Ernest Orlando Lawrence.* 1968. (Out of print.)

Davis, Nuel P. *Lawrence and Oppenheimer.* Simon & Schuster, 1968.

Driemen, J.E. *Robert Oppenheimer: Atomic Dawn: A Biography of Robert Oppenheimer.* MacMillan Children's Book Group, 1988.

Fahey, Joseph J. & Armstrong, Richard. *A Peace Reader: Essential Readings on War, Justice, Non-Violence, and World Order.* Paulist Press, 1992.

Farris, John. *Hiroshima.* Lucent Books, 1990.

Feis, H. *The Atomic Bomb & the End of World War II.* Princeton University Press, 1961.

Fermi, Laura. *Atoms in the Family: My Life with Enrico Fermi.* U. New Mexico Press, 1954.

Frisch, Otto. *What Little I Remember.* Cambridge U. Press, 1991.

Giovannitti, Len & Freed, Fred. *The Decision to Drop the Bomb.* Coward-McCann, 1965. (Out of print.)

Goodchild, Peter J. *J. Robert Oppenheimer: Shatterer of Worlds.* Fromm International Pub., 1985.

Gottfried, Ted. *Enrico Fermi.* Facts on File, 1992.

Groves, Leslie M. *Now It Can Be Told: The Story of the Manhattan Project.* Da Capo Press, 1962. (Currently out of print.)

Hewlett, Richard G. & Duncan, Francis. *Atomic Shield: A History of the United States Atomic Energy Commission, 1947-1952.* U. California Press, 1990.

Hirschfeld, Burt. *A Cloud Over Hiroshima.* Julian Messner, 1967. (Out of print.)

Hoddeson, Lillian & Henriksen, Paul W. & Meade, Roger A. *Critical Assembly: A Technical History of Los Alamos During the Oppenheimer Years, 1943-1945.* Cambridge U. Press, 1993.

Irving, David. *The German Atomic Bomb.* Da Capo Press, 1967.

Irving, David. *The German Atomic Bomb: The History of Nuclear Research in Nazi Germany.* Da Capo Press, 1983.

Jagger, J. *The Nuclear Lion: What Every Citizen Should Know About Nuclear Power & Nuclear War.* Plenum Pub. Corp., 1991.

Jette, Eleanor. *Inside Box 1663.* Los Alamos Historical Society, 1977.

Jungk, Robert. *Children of the Ashes.* Harcourt, Brace Jovanovich, 1961.

Kuneta, James W. *City of Fire: Los Alamos and the Birth of the Atomic Age. 1943-1945.* Prentice-Hall, 1978.

Lamont, Lansing. *Day of Trinity.* Atheneum, 1985. (Out of print.)

Lanouette, William & Silard, Bela. *Genius in the Shadows: A Biography of Leo Szilard. the Man Behind the Bomb.* MacMillan Pub., 1993.

Laurence, William L. *Dawn Over Zero: The Story of the Atomic Bomb.* Greenwood Press, 1972.

Laurence, William L. *The Hell Bomb.* Alfred. A. Knoff, 1951. (Out of print.)

Lee, Steven P. *Morality, Prudence, and Nuclear Weapons.* Cambridge U. Press, 1993.

Lindsay, James M. *Congress and Nuclear Weapons.* Johns Hopkins U. Press, 1991.

Lyon, F. & Evans, J., ed. *Los Alamos: The First Forty Years.* Los Alamos Historical Society, 1984. (Out of print.)

Marx, Joseph L. *Nagasaki: The Necessary Bomb?* MacMillan Co., 1971. (Out of print.)

Marx, Joseph L. *Seven Hours to Zero.* G.P. Putman & Sons, 1967. (Out of print.)

Morimoto, Junko. *My Hiroshima.* Puffin Books, 1992.

O'Neal, Michael. *President Truman and the Atomic Bomb: Opposing Viewpoints.* Greenhaven Press, 1990.

Oppenheimer, J. Robert. *Atom and Void: Essays on Science and Community*. Princeton U. Press, 1980.

Osada, A. *Children of the A-Bomb*. G.P. Putman & Sons, 1963. (Out of print.)

Oughterson, H.W. & Warren, S., eds. *Medical Effects of the Atomic Bomb in Japan*. McGraw-Hill, 1956. (Out of print.)

Powers, Thomas. *Heisenberg's War: The Secret History of the German Bomb*. Little, Brown, 1994.

Rhodes, Richard. *The Making of the Atomic Bomb*. Simon & Schuster, 1987.

Rosenthal, Deborah. *Heart of the Bomb: the Dangerous Allure of Weapons Work*. Addison-Wesley Inc., 1990.

Rossi, Bruno. *Moments in the Life of a Scientist*. Cambridge U. Press, 1990,

Rummel, Jack. *Robert Oppenheimer: Dark Prince*. Facts on File, 1992.

Russ, Harlow W. *Project Alberta: The Preparation of Atomic Bombs for Use in World War II*. Exceptional Books, 1990.

Schneir, Walter. *Invitation to an Inquest*. Doubleday, 1965. (Out of print.)

Segre, Emilio. *Mind Always in Motion: The Autobiography of Emilio Segre*. U. California Press, 1993.

Serber, Charlotte & Wilson, Jane S. *Standing By and Making Do: Women of Wartime Los Alamos*. Los Alamos Historical Society, 1988.

Shepley, J.R. & Blair, C. Jr. *The Hydrogen Bomb: The Men, the Menace, the Mechanism*. Greenwood, 1954.

Skates, John R. *The Invasion of Japan: Alternative to the Bomb*. U. South Carolina Press, 1994.

Smyth, Henry D. *Atomic Energy for Military Purposes: The Official Report on the Development of the Atomic Bomb under the Auspices of the United States Government, 1940-1945*. Stanford U. Press, 1990.

Snow, C.P. *The Now Men*. MacMillan Press, 1959. (Out of print.)

Stern, Philip. *The Oppenheimer Case: Security on Trial*. Harper & Row, 1969. (Out of print.)

Strauss, Lewis. *Men and Decisions*. Doubleday & Co., 1962.

Szasz, Ferenc M. *The Day the Sun Rose Twice: The Story of the Trinity Site Explosion, July 16, 1945*. U. New Mexico Press, 1984.

Teller, Edward & Brown, Allen. *The Legacy of Hiroshima*. Greenwood Pub. Group, 1962.

Tibbets, Paul W. *Flight of the Enola Gay*. Buckeye Aviation Book Co., 1989.

Ulam, Stanislaw. *Adventures of a Mathematician*. University of California, 1991.

Wyder, Peter. *Day One*. Simon & Schuster, 1984.

York, Herbert. *The Advisors: Oppenheimer, Teller and the Superbomb*. Stanford U. Press, 1976.

Zaloga, Steven J. *Target America: The Soviet Union and the Strategic Arms Race, 1945 to 1964*. Presido Press, 1993.

(This bibliography is not a complete list. For a more complete list visit your public library or refer to the bibliographies of some of the books listed above, especially those with recent publication dates.)

# BIBLIOGRAPHY—VIDEOS

*The Atomic Bomb.* Best Film & Video, 1970.

*Atomic Cafe.* First Run.

*Atomic Stampede.* U. Utah Press, 1994.

*The Day After Trinity.* Pyramid Home Video, 1981.

*General Paul Tibbets: Reflections on Hiroshima.* Buckeye Aviation Book Co., 1989.

*The Hydrogen Bomb.* Best Film & Video Corp., 1975.

*Remembering Los Alamos: World War II.* Los Alamos Historical Society, 1993.

## About the Author

Jim Clayton is currently a writer and ski instructor living in Taos, New Mexico. He has a degree in Theatre Arts from the famed Pasadena Playhouse College of Theatre Arts where he once acted with Dustin Hoffman. He has spent most of his adult life in the computer field in Los Angeles, Cincinnati, Connecticut, New York City and Atlanta. He now spends most of his time as a ski instructor, writer, writing consultant, tennis instructor and traveler. He is currently working on several books (including a book of poems) and a play. He is already considering a sequel to this book.